PUTTING IT ALL TOGETHER

• TEACHING THE RESEARCH PROCESS •

Diana Barnett

UpstartBooks

Janesville, Wisconsin

Published by UpstartBooks
401 S. Wright Road
Janesville, WI 53547

1-800-448-4887

© Diana Barnett, 2009
Cover design: Debra Neu

The paper used in this publication meets the minimum requirements of American National
Standard for Information Science — Permanence of Paper for Printed Library Material.
ANSI/NISO Z39.48-1992.

Table of Contents

Introduction

Tackling an informational problem is an exciting process. It involves an important set of skills that each of us will use over and over again as long as we need to find answers to questions that we have. Research can be as simple as discovering which cell phone best suits your needs or as complicated as deciding which treatment is the best choice for a particular type of cancer. A research project, then, is a presentation of one's own thinking backed up by the ideas or information of others in the field. It is a collection of components or pieces, as in a puzzle, that is brought together to form a whole thought.

In order to come up with the best solution to your problem, you must analyze a variety of informational sources, and make some assumptions based on what you have learned. Just as you have friends that offer you different kinds of advice and you listen to several options before you make a decision, research is the same process. We will gather several pieces of information, think about what each has to offer, and determine a solution to our informational problem.

There are prerequisite skills that students must be exposed to and allowed to practice before embarking on a full-blown research project if they are to be successful. First, they need to clearly understand any task they are asked to do. They must be able to identify what kind of information they need. They need to be familiar with various informational sources in order to do this. They need know how to locate the sources, and from these select the best sources for the information they need. They must be able to find information within these sources, and determine which parts are actually relevant for their project. They need to know how to collect and organize information from multiple sources. Students will need to present their results in an appropriate format. Lastly, they need to evaluate their work according to a prescribed rubric that the teacher has provided at the beginning of the project.

Research projects can be overwhelming tasks. It is important that students have practice using the prerequisite skills noted above over a period of grade levels a little at a time. If students are to be effective users of information, they must be provided with effective modeling and guided practice throughout their educational journey.

Researching information should be enjoyable. There is nothing more challenging than discovering a solution based on one's own research. In the process, students will find they have become mini-experts on their topics and will gain valuable skills they need to become lifelong learners.

This book will take you and your students through the research process. Organized by individual components of the process, you'll find suggestions for teacher modeling, followed by activities to be practiced by students. Also included are pages designed to share with students, indicated with a "Share with Students" icon. These pages may be used as reproducible handouts or projected for the entire class. What you choose to use will depend on the experience level of your students in the research process. It is hoped that this guide will assist you and your students in putting all the components together to create a meaningful learning project.

Using Information Effectively Is a Critical, Lifelong Skill

Learning is all about standards, because we are accountable for teaching students critical skills that are essential. The American Association of School Librarians has identified nine standards of information literacy for student learning:

Information Literacy

- **Standard 1:** The student who is information literate accesses information efficiently and effectively.

- **Standard 2:** The student who is information literate evaluates information critically and competently.

- **Standard 3:** The student who is information literate uses information accurately and creatively.

Independent Learning

- **Standard 4:** The student who is an independent learner is information literate and pursues information related to personal interests.

- **Standard 5:** The student who is an independent learner is information literate and appreciates literature and other creative expressions of information.

- **Standard 6:** The student who is an independent learner is information literate and strives for excellence in information seeking and knowledge generation.

Social Responsibility

- **Standard 7:** The student who contributes positively to the learning community and to society is information literate and recognizes the importance of information to a democratic society.

- **Standard 8:** The student who contributes positively to the learning community and to society is information literate and practices ethical behavior in regard to information and information technology.

- **Standard 9:** The student who contributes positively to the learning community and society is information literate and participates effectively in groups to pursue and generate information.

Teaching the Research Process

Synthesis: "An integration of two or more elements, which results in a new creation."
—*American Heritage Dictionary*

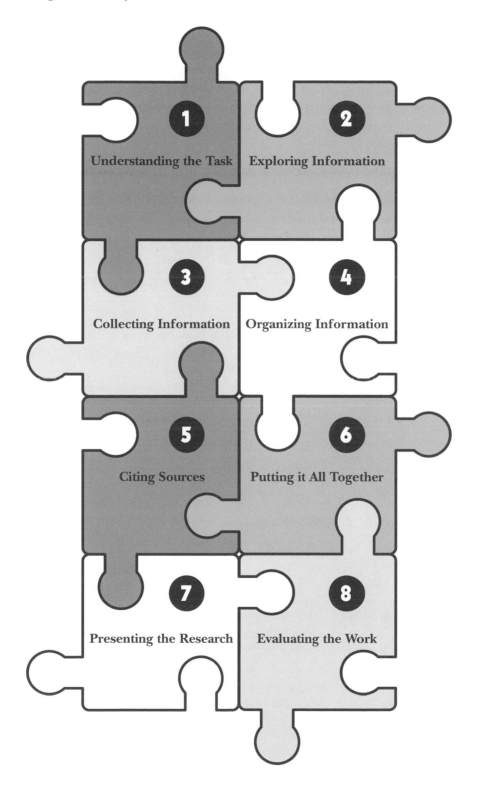

1. Understanding the Task
2. Exploring Information
3. Collecting Information
4. Organizing Information
5. Citing Sources
6. Putting it All Together
7. Presenting the Research
8. Evaluating the Work

Understanding the Task

How successful students are in the research process is determined by the level of understanding they have about their assignment. The National Standards call for students to "research a topic using a variety of sources." Research can be very overwhelming because of the higher cognitive demand required to plan a strategy, locate and evaluate information, and put all of the pieces together in a final product. It is a multi-step process that students are expected to conduct independently. Therefore, it is imperative that teachers clearly explain each step of the process and model those steps for students.

Introducing the Rubric

The best way to approach a research project is to begin with the end in mind. Discuss with students exactly what is required and what is expected. A rubric that clearly describes what is expected in order for students to be proficient in the research process is a necessary guide so they know they are on the right track during their work. A sample rubric is included on page 9. As you discuss the rubric, allow students to look at examples of quality research projects. They must be exposed to work that meets high expectations if they are to clearly understand their task.

Additional Sources for Developing Rubrics:

www.psych.westminster.edu/inquiry1g/comparison_rubric.html

www.usd305.com/staffdev/hs/ss/ssrubrics.htm

school.discovery.com/schrockguide/assess.html

rubistar.4teachers.org/index.php

intranet.cps.k12.il.us/Assessments/Ideas_and_Rubrics/Rubric_Bank/rubric_bank.html

www.teach-nology.com/web_tools/rubrics/

www.sdcoe.k12.ca.us/score/actbank/trubrics.htm

www.ncsu.edu/midlink/ho.html

www.uwstout.edu/soe/profdev/rubrics.shtml

www.tcet.unt.edu/START/instruct/general/rubrics.htm

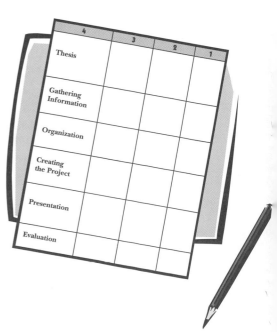

Research Project Rubric

	4	3	2	1
Thesis The thesis statement is well thought out, clear, and focused. The informational problem is challenging and requires higher-level thinking skills to tackle. It was determined that adequate resources were available to thoroughly research this thesis.	Student created a focused thesis statement that requires moderately high-level thinking skills to research.	The thesis statement is underdeveloped or unclear. Required teacher assistance.	Student was unable to come up with a research question or thesis statement.
Gathering Information Student gathered information from a variety of quality resources, including print and electronic information from approved databases. Was able to make revisions when needed.	Student used many resources, both print and electronic, to find information that addressed thesis. Made revisions with teacher assistance.	Student relied on one or more resources to research the thesis statement. Needed revisions were not made.	Student did not focus on information gathering process. Information was incomplete.
Organization Student carefully selected appropriate information that related to the thesis, including supporting details. Thoughts were well organized and stated from the student's perspective.	Student selected and organized information that addressed the thesis with relatively few errors.	Student attempted to organize the information, but made some errors. Had difficulty in selecting resources to support thesis.	Student was unable to organize the information located.
Creating the Project Student used information from a variety of sources in a well-organized structure to create an original product that clearly communicated the thesis with accuracy, detail, and understanding.	Student's product dealt with the thesis in a way that showed learning using some detail and accuracy.	Student needed more effort to create a complete project. Information did not support the thesis well.	Student's work is incomplete and not logically organized.
Presentation Delivery mode effectively communicates the writer's message in a well-organized, creative manner. All sources (print, visual, and sound) are documented consistently within the text and on the Works Cited page.	Delivery communicated the writer's message in an organized manner. Sources were documented both within the text and on the Works Cited page with few errors.	Delivery method was not effective in communicating student's ideas. Additional work is required.	Student did not have an understanding of the process. Delivery mode was not effective, and information was undocumented.
Evaluation Student thoughtfully and accurately reflects on personal effort and quality of work completed.	Student completed an evaluation of personal effort and quality of work completed.	Student completed an evaluation of personal effort and quality work with little understanding of the process.	Evaluation was incomplete.

Understanding the Task
Focus of the Task

The starting point is the focus of the task. Are topics assigned? May students select a topic? What are the topic parameters? Regardless of the way the topic is approached, students need practice in working with a topic to make it "research-friendly."

Students in a science class, for example, may be asked to choose a disease and research the various treatment options available. The first step is to identify a disease: *Coronary Heart Disease.* The next step is to state the informational problem to be researched: *Although coronary heart disease is a serious problem, a range of treatments is available to patients who suffer from this affliction.* In this case, the teacher has identified the task and its parameters. The student needs to choose a disease and create a statement that actually describes the whole focus of his research. This statement is called a **thesis statement.** The student should refer to it often during the research process to make sure he or she remains focused on the informational problem. The more clear the thesis statement, the easier it will be to evaluate and determine the best informational sources for the research.

Understanding the Task

- Explain to students that together you will brainstorm ideas to research and will end by creating a statement that guides the direction of a possible research project.

- Select a general topic that you chose or use an idea from a student.

- Write that topic on the board.

- Ask students to think of questions they have about the topic. Write those on the board or on an overhead transparency.

- Have students create statements from the questions that could become a thesis for a possible research project. Write those statements next to the questions.

Topic Idea: High School Graduation Requirements

Questions:

- Why do schools require so many credits for graduation?

  Although many schools have recently increased the number of credits for graduation, high schools require too many credits for graduation from their students.

- Why are credits required in so many subject areas?

  High school graduation requirements should focus on the basics of mathematics and language arts in order to have the skills to enter the workforce or college.

- Should everyone have the same graduation requirements?

  Rather than a "one plan fits all" system, high school graduation requirements should depend on individual abilities and future plans.

- Are high school students well prepared when they graduate?

  Even though students in foreign countries are compared with students in the United States, high school students in America are well prepared for college or entering the work force when they graduate.

- Should graduation requirements be more rigorous?

  To ensure that everyone is prepared for his/her future, high school graduation requirements for students in America should be more rigorous.

Talk about each statement.

- Is the statement one that could be argued? Is the statement more than just opinion?
- Is it a topic that could be researched? What resources would be best to use to locate information?
- Is it specific and focused, avoiding words such as "all"?
- Does it provide a guideline to follow for those reading the research?
- Can the thesis be adequately developed in the required length of the project?

Have students form groups and practice this process.

Additional Resources for Developing a Thesis

The following Web sites provide more practice for students in creating and developing a thesis for their research project.

Technology Note: Using a projection device, these Web sites can provide further brainstorming opportunities for the entire class or small groups of students who need more practice in generating their thesis statements.

Purdue OWL

owl.english.purdue.edu/workshops/hypertext/ResearchW/thesis.html

Harvard University

www.fas.harvard.edu/~wricntr/documents/Thesis.html

Understanding the Task

What do I need to know?

Standard: Students use strategies to generate ideas for written work or presentations—developing a focus.

Activity: Organize students into small groups, with the teacher assigning a different general topic to each group. Ask students to brainstorm questions they might want to find out about their topic. After they generate several questions, they choose one and create a statement that can serve as a main focus for their research.

Sample: Divide students randomly into groups of four or five. Each group works on one of five different topics. For example, topics such as drug testing in schools, school uniforms, paying to participate in extracurricular activities, graduation requirements, and early graduation could be used. Each group appoints a recorder to document work accomplished. The group generates questions about their topic. After they have listed several questions, they choose one question that they feel is the most interesting or controversial, and create a statement from it that could be the focus of a research project. When everyone is finished, each group reports to the class.

Understanding the Task

Names: _____

Your topic: _____

Your questions:

Circle the question you chose to use to create your focus statement.

_____

_____

_____

_____

_____

_____

Your focus statement:

_____

_____

_____

_____

_____

Recorder Signature _____

Understanding the Task
Recognizing Thesis Statements

Teacher Modeling Idea 2

Standard: Students use strategies to generate ideas for written work or presentations—determining the main idea.

Activity: As a class, read the article about increased graduation requirements in Missouri schools. Discuss the thesis of the article. Have students list all of the information mentioned in the article that supports the main idea. Note that the key words that were used in the initial search for this article "high school graduation requirements," are highlighted in the text of the article. Many databases use this technique to guide students to the most relevant parts of the article they are reading.

Missouri Board Raises Graduation Standards Article

Title: *Missouri Board Raises Graduation Standards.*, By: Viadero, Debra, Education Week, 02774232, 10/19/2005, Vol. 25, Issue 8

Database: *Academic Search Elite*

Missouri Board Raises Graduation Standards

Section: STATE CAPITALS: NEWS IN BRIEF

Missouri's state board of education has voted to raise high school graduation requirements for the state's 900,000 public school students.

Approved on Oct. 6, the changes are the first the state has made to its graduation rules in 20 years. The new requirements raise the number of credits required for graduation from 22 to 24, and mandate new classes in personal finance and health.

Under the rules, students beginning with the class of 2010 will have to earn four credits in English, three each in mathematics, science, and social studies, and half a credit each in personal finance and health.

Jim Morris, a Missouri education department spokesman, said the changes, when proposed by the board, drew 600 public comments, most of which favored the plan.

The new rules are part of an ongoing effort across Missouri to raise the rigor of high school academics and align the state's requirements with those of local districts. Department officials estimate that 70 percent of students are in high schools that already require 24 credits for graduation.

By Debra Viadero

Source: Education Week, 10/19/2005, Vol. 25 Issue 8, p18, 1p

Item: 18703479

Understanding the Task
Recognizing Thesis Statements

Standard: Students use strategies to generate ideas for written work or presentations—developing a focus.

Activity: Independently read a news article reprinted from the *Minneapolis Star Tribune* and ProQuest Database about graduation requirements. List the sentence below that guides the information of the entire article. Then list sentences that give details to support the main idea.

List the sentence that states the main idea of this article.

_____

_____

_____

_____

List sentences that show evidence that supports the main idea.

_____

_____

_____

_____

_____

_____

_____

_____

Article: Missouri Board Raises Graduation Standards

More emphasis on math, science: Leaders rightly push for expanded, rigorous K–12 programs. *Minneapolis Star Tribune*, 07-23-2006.

RSEC:

During a recent forum on academic competitiveness, Intel board chair and former CEO Craig Barrett called the world his company's recruiting pool. When his managers need engineers and scientists, searches don't stop at U.S. borders; the best and brightest workers can come from Shreveport or Shanghai, Minneapolis or Mumbai.

Yet Barrett worries that American presence in that worker pool is small and shrinking because our schools aren't preparing enough students. Asian and European nations require more math and science of their students—and that emphasis shows when they choose careers.

A survey of Minnesota student interests highlights the problem. According to an assessment of more than 91,000 eighth- and tenth-graders last year, only 11 percent of the middle schoolers and 21 percent of sophomores are interested in careers in technology, math, and science.

Those percentages need to rise. State estimates predict that 20 to 33 percent of future job growth will be in technical fields. If local students want a shot at those positions, they must study higher level math and science.

To make that happen, Gov. Tim Pawlenty and the state Department of Education have a number of promising plans in the works. Under the governor's Science, Technology, Engineering and Math (STEM) initiative, more rigorous goals are being developed for student achievement. The legislature agreed to bump up math and science requirements for high school graduation, increase funding for IB and AP programs and fund Minnesota's participation in an international study of math and science achievement. Just last week, a U.S.-based software company agreed to provide free mechanical engineering and design software to Minnesota schools.

Even students who don't choose technical careers can benefit from a more rigorous curriculum because many of the jobs they'll seek require strong problem-solving and reasoning skills. State leaders have the best interests of students and Minnesota's economic future in mind in promoting this educational focus. STEM merits strong support and participation.

Exploring the Information

As with any assignment, we want to discover what students already know about any lesson we are about to teach. That will determine where we need to begin, and which prerequisite skills students will need to learn. Some students will already be familiar with several informational sources, and they can become guides for students who don't have these experiences.

Brainstorming types of sources for a particular topic is a great way to get students thinking about resources that are available. Some good questions to ask about the selected topic are: Is historical or background information needed? Does information need to be current? Does the information need to be from a particular geographic location? Is technical information found in graphs and charts needed?

Once a list of sources has been determined through the brainstorming process in Student Exercise 2, the library media specialist can step in to add to that list. A list of possible sources for student use is included on pages 20–21.

Once the list of possible sources is created, students then need to decide which of those sources are best suited for the topic they have selected. Again, questions like the ones listed above can help students narrow their list to relevant sources of information. It is difficult for students to understand which source might be the better choice without some practice. Brief exercises in comparing the treatment of the same information from source to source will provide experience using these materials, and allow students to make a better determination on what will be the most useful for their research project.

The second part of working with information is actually locating the sources physically or electronically, and finding the information within those sources. Where are materials located? Can the information be found in the classroom, in databases located on the computer, or in the media center? If the source is a person, can they be reached by telephone, e-mail, or a personal visit? Students need lots of opportunities to practice using a variety of resources in order to be efficient users of information.

Exploring Information

Information literacy is defined as the ability to know when there is a need for information, and to be able to identify, locate, evaluate, and effectively use that information for the issue or problem at hand.

—National Forum on Information Literacy

Now that you have taken a closer look at your selected topic, you'll need to decide what types of informational sources are best suited to research the information you will need.

What informational sources are out there?

Do you need historical information or a basic overview of a subject?

- You might take a look at general *(World Book Encyclopedia)* and specialized encyclopedias *(Encyclopedia of Science and Technology)*. Encyclopedias provide background information on thousands of subjects. This may be the best place to start in order to find out general knowledge about your topic.

- Nonfiction books *(The Man Who Made Time Travel)* on your subject may be helpful. The card catalog at your school library media center or local library can help you locate titles on your topic.

- Periodicals, such as magazines, journals, and newspapers can also give overview or background information on your topic. Look in online databases such as InfoTrac, Electric Library, and Newsbank to locate magazines *(Newsweek, Sports Illustrated)*, journals *(Journal of the American Medical Association)*, and newspapers *(New York Times, Baltimore Sun)*. These may be found online or in hard copy. Ask your media specialist for databases available at your school or local library.

Do you need current information on a topic?

- Periodicals (magazines and newspapers) provide up-to-date information on lots of topics. Because these sources are published either daily or monthly, they are often more current than books. Look in your media center databases.

- Recognized organizations (American Heart Association, National Aeronautics and Space Administration) often provide helpful Web sites with a variety of information including news articles, research, graphs, tables, and charts. Many Web sites allow students to send an online inquiry to a professional from that organization.

Do you need information about your state and community?

- Nonfiction books *(Roadside History of Wyoming, Ghosts on the Range: Eerie True Tales of Wyoming, Detroit's Michigan Central Station)* on your town or state are usually available at your school, community, or college library. Ask your media specialist about a loan service through which you may obtain books on your topic that are available in other locations in your state.

- Local and state organizations can provide a wealth of information about your community and your state. Local historical societies, government agencies, and social service organizations can provide information on many issues in your area. A list of local organizations is available in the phone directory or from your community library or chamber of commerce.

- Professionals living in your community can be valuable resources of information on local issues. Individuals involved in local or state government, social service organizations, or a particular business can provide information that will assist you in your research.

- Local, state, and regional newspapers provide some of the best coverage of local issues. Many local newspaper offices archive and index their newspapers and many are now online with archival searches on various topics. One of the best free Web sites for newspaper searches is LibrarySpot (www.libraryspot.com), which allows you to locate newspapers by state and city.

Do you need audio or visual information on your topic?

- Slides, video, or DVD recordings are available in school media centers, classrooms, and college and community libraries on various topics. Programs you view at home can also be good resources for your research. National Public Television and National Public Radio are excellent sources of quality programming on a variety of subjects. A listing of available programs in your area may be obtained from Web sites for these two organizations.

- Many graphics and photos are available on the Internet. Many require written permission in order for you to use these, even in a school assignment. It is a good idea to e-mail the author of the item you would like to use and ask permission. In every case, you should give credit to the photographer, artist, or author of any type of information you include as part of your research project.

- Original photographs, as well as other graphics that you create yourself can be a great addition to a research project. These can be computer-generated or taken with a digital camera.

Exploring the Information
Examining an Informational Source

Explain to students that they will brainstorm a list of informational sources that will assist them with a research project. Remain in the classroom to do this activity.

Use the example of a student textbook. Have students look at their own copy as you point out the features and information contained in this book. Look at the table of contents. Ask students what kinds of information are provided in the book. Examine the index and glossary. If a bibliography is included, talk about its purpose with students. Look for information about the authors of the book. What are their qualifications that make the information reliable?

Exploring the Information

What informational sources are available to me?

Checking for Background Knowledge of Informational Sources

Teacher Modeling Idea 2

After a discussion on general reference sources students have already learned to use, explain to students they will be organized into small groups in the media center, with table space for examining various resources. Each student is given the following handout and asked to write the names of the different resources on their sheet.

Sample: Students are divided randomly into groups of four or five. Students may move about the media center as they look for different sources. Each student in the group records a list of the resources on his or her individual worksheet. Students may ask the media specialist for assistance in understanding a particular resource. When the time is up, each group is asked for their list of potential sources for research, and those are listed on the board. Students can add any additional resources to their list that have been shared by other groups. When the activity is finished, students will have a list of potential resources for their research project.

Exploring the Information

Checking for Background Knowledge of Informational Sources

Student Exercise 2 Worksheet

Names: _____

List all informational sources located in the media center that could assist you with a research project:

_____

_____

_____

_____

_____

_____

_____

List additional informational sources that were not on your list.

_____

_____

_____

_____

Learning About Informational Sources
Which Sources Should I Use?

Discuss the variety of sources students discovered in Exercise 2. Focus on a general encyclopedia and examine the coverage of the term "school." How in-depth is the information? Can they find information about current issues dealing with schools?

Explain to students they will examine a variety of informational sources and rate them based on how well each source helps solve an informational problem. Place them in small groups with table space to work in the media center. On each table, place a copy of a general encyclopedia, an almanac, an atlas, a news magazine, and a local newspaper. Ask students to rate each source when used to find material on the following informational problems:

- Find the top three countries with the highest number of people who die each year.

- Learn about crimes that took place in your community in the past two weeks.

- Read and discuss one event that involved the president of the United States recently.

- Locate and list all the states that border your state.

- Compare the flags of Sweden and Denmark.

Learning About Informational Sources

Names: _____

Using the informational sources provided for you (encyclopedia, almanac, atlas, local newspaper, and news magazine), rate each, and comment on its ability to help you solve the following informational problems:

1. Find the top three countries with the highest number of people who die each year.
2. Learn about crimes that took place in your community in the past two weeks.
3. Read and discuss one event that involved the president of the United States recently.
4. Locate and list all the states that border your state.
5. Compare the flags of Sweden and Denmark.

Atlas			
Problem #	**Found Easily**	**Not Helpful**	**Comments**
1			
2			
3			
4			
5			

Almanac			
Problem #	**Found Easily**	**Not Helpful**	**Comments**
1			
2			
3			
4			
5			

Newspaper			
Problem #	Found Easily	Not Helpful	Comments
1			
2			
3			
4			
5			

Encyclopedia			
Problem #	Found Easily	Not Helpful	Comments
1			
2			
3			
4			
5			

News Magazine			
Problem #	Found Easily	Not Helpful	Comments
1			
2			
3			
4			
5			

Using the Internet

Technology can make information gathering much easier—if you can tell the difference between meaningful, useful information and the kind that's not. You type in a search term, and often hundreds of informational sources are at your fingertips. Which resources provide reliable information for your research? Because anyone can publish anything on the Internet at anytime, it is necessary to evaluate Web sites before using information from them. This is an important part of the research process. Information used for research must be accurate, reliable, and unbiased. Use the following guide to evaluate Web sites. It is also helpful to evaluate other sources, as well.

Authority

Who is the author?

What are his/her qualifications?

Is the author affiliated with a recognized institution or organization?

Examining the address (URL) of the Web site can offer valuable information on its reliability. The host, a three-letter code, tells what type of domain is represented.

.edu: college or university (http://www.umich.edu)

.gov: government agency or organization (http://www.irs.gov)

.com: commercial organization (http://www.cnn.com)

.net: network provider (http://www.verizon.net)

.org: nonprofit organization (http://www.unitedway.org)

.int: intergovernmental organization (http://www.who.int)

.mil: military (http://www.army.mil)

.info: general information site (http://www.microbes.info)

Accuracy

Is the information correct?

Can the information be checked out through other sources?

Reliability

Is the information dependable?

Are sources stated to back up the text?

Objectivity

Is the material unbiased?

Is the writer trying to persuade us about something?

Date

When was the information created?

When was the information updated?

Is it current enough for your research?

Usability

Does it address your research thesis? Can you understand the information?

Is the site organized in a logical manner so it is easy to find information?

Is the material approached from a research base or is it more popular in nature?

Evaluating Information: The Internet

Because Web sites are so overwhelming, it is often difficult for students to determine the credibility of the author, if the information is biased, etc. Sometimes the ending of the URL can be the best clue to the suitability of the Web site for student information gathering. Display the list of URL endings from page 28 for students, and share examples of each with them.

.edu   This appears in any URL for an institution of higher learning, which generally has dependable information. Log on to Purdue University's Web site, www.purdue.edu, for an example and explore what information is available and discuss why this would be reliable information.

.gov   Show students the NASA Web site, www.nasa.gov, and point out the author's name and updated Web site date at the bottom of the homepage. NASA's Web site is updated daily. Discuss why a government-sponsored Web site would provide factual information.

.com   Although Web sites ending with ".com" are commercial sites, many are very useful. Newspaper sites, and often library sites, have this URL ending. Share the *New York Times* Web site, www.nyt.com, with your students, and discuss how they might use this information in their research. Although newspapers actually make money selling ads more than subscriptions, their coverage should be objective except for the editorial section.

.net   Beware of sites with this URL ending. As mentioned before, anyone with an Internet service provider can have a Web site. Have students examine the Web site www. zapatopi.net. There is a link on this page to an article on the tree octopus. Ask students to evaluate it for reliability. At first glance, it appears there may be some credibility to this information. Have them use their background information. What do they know about the octopus and its habitat? Could this creature really exist? A quick glance at the rest of the Web site reveals a collection of imaginative, but nonexistent creatures and unsubstantiated "facts." Share with students that to use information from these Web sites is not acceptable.

.org   These Web sites generally represent nonprofit organizations, which often provide useful information for researchers. Sites like National Public Television, www.npt.org, are good sources for students. Similar sites like the National Wildlife Federation, www.nwf. org, and the Sierra Club, www.sierraclub.org, provide helpful information, but also have a bias toward the focus of their organization. These Web sites may provide a good discussion about the purpose of various organizations and how information on their sites must be evaluated for point of view.

.int   We don't run into these sites too often in school research, but international org̶ nizations like the World Health Organization, www.who.int, can provide very valuabl̶ information online.

.mil   Because there is a wealth of military information, the armed forces have individu-al Web sites that are government affiliated. A good example is www.marines.mil.

.info   Web sites with this ending often provide collections of information in one site to make researching easier. A good example is www.microbes.info, which combines numer-ous links on microbiology.

Evaluating a Source

Explain to students that you are going to evaluate an informational source together. Select an informational book and run it through the following criteria to determine its suitability for research purposes.

Authority

Who is the author?

What are his/her qualifications?

Is the author affiliated with a recognized institution or organization?

Accuracy

Is the information correct?

Can the information be checked out through other sources?

Reliability

Is the information dependable?

Are sources stated to back up the text?

Objectivity

Is the material unbiased?

Is the writer trying to persuade us about something?

Date

When was the information created?

When was the information updated?

Is it current enough for your research?

Usability

Does it address your research thesis? Can you understand the information?

Is the source organized in a logical manner so it is easy to find information?

Is the material approached from a research base or is it more popular in nature?

Evaluating a Source

Using a resource that you have located as a possible source of information for your research project, apply the following criteria to see if it passes the test of being a reliable source of information.

Authority

Who is the author? _____

What are his/her qualifications? _____

Is the author affiliated with a recognized institution or organization? _____

Accuracy

Is the information correct? _____

Can the information be checked out through other sources? _____

Reliability

Is the information dependable? _____

Are sources stated to back up the text? _____

Objectivity

Is the material unbiased? _____

Is the writer trying to persuade us about something? _____

Date

When was the information created? _____

When was the information updated? _____

Is it current enough for your research? _____

Usability

Does it address your research thesis? Can you understand the information?

_____

Is the source organized in a logical manner so it is easy to find information?

_____

Is the material approached from a research base or is it more popular in nature?

_____

Evaluating a Web Site

Discuss the variety of information and types of sites available on the Internet. Explain the criteria for posting a site on the Web. Choose a Web site, and together evaluate its potential as a viable resource by answering the following questions.

Authority

Who is the author?

What are his/her qualifications?

Is the author affiliated with a recognized institution or organization?

Accuracy

Is the information correct?

Can the information be checked out through other sources?

Reliability

Is the information dependable?

Are sources stated to back up the text?

Objectivity

Is the material unbiased?

Is the writer trying to persuade us about something?

Date

When was the information created?

When was the information updated?

Is it current enough for your research?

Usability

Does it address your research thesis? Can you understand the information?

Is the site organized in a logical manner so it is easy to find information?

Is the material approached from a research base or is it more popular in nature?

Evaluating a Web Site

Using a Web site you have selected as a possible informational resource for your research project, evaluate it based on the following criteria:

Authority

Who is the author? _____

What are his/her qualifications? _____

Is the author affiliated with a recognized institution or organization? _____

Accuracy

Is the information correct? _____

Can the information be checked out through other sources? _____

Reliability

Is the information dependable? _____

Are sources stated to back up the text? _____

Objectivity

Is the material unbiased? _____

Is the writer trying to persuade us about something? _____

Date

When was the information created? _____

When was the information updated? _____

Is it current enough for your research? _____

Usability

Does it address your research thesis? Can you understand the information?

_____

Is the site organized in a logical manner so it is easy to find information?

_____

Is the material approached from a research base or is it more popular in nature?

_____

Collecting the Information

When sources with useful information have been located, it is time to glean the relevant portions that will be helpful for the student project. Students should refer to their thesis statements to determine what information will be helpful to support it. It is helpful to write five or six questions, based on the thesis statement, whose answers will directly support the thesis. This will help students know what to write in note form and what to discard.

Once students have a clear idea of the information they will need to support the thesis, they will need to write down those main ideas from their reading in an organized, consistent manner. When students are able to make copies of information, such as periodical articles, they may highlight key points, quotes they'd like to use, and information needed for their bibliography. It is easy to transfer this information to note cards that can be easily organized when preparing to create the first draft of their project.

As students are recording relevant information from which to create the draft of their projects, they should also record information to be included in the bibliography. This is a good time to introduce the citation process and provide the formula (MLA or APA format) students are expected to follow to complete a bibliography or works cited page. Use the guidelines for citations in the section, "Citing Sources: Giving Credit Where Credit is Due," with students as they begin this stage of the process.

A discussion on plagiarism is appropriate before embarking on note taking of relevant information. Show students examples of powerful direct quotations, how they add to a final presentation of information, and how students must document the source of this type of material.

Again, a research project is a complicated task. Students must have many opportunities to practice the various components of the research process throughout the grade levels and prior to a major research assignment to guarantee success.

Collecting the Information

Let's return to the sample thesis statements on high school graduation for brainstorming purposes. Write the following statement on the board or overhead transparency, and tell students this is what you are trying to prove with your research:

In order to be competitive in the job market, American high school students, regardless of ability or future plans, should participate in a challenging curriculum with rigorous graduation requirements.

Brainstorm with your students some questions you would need answers to in order to prove this thesis.

- It is said that college entrance exam scores are being compared worldwide and scores of American students are often lower. What are the graduation requirements of students in European countries? In Asian countries?

- How well does a system that requires the same courses from all students prepare students for college? For the workplace?

- Are some schools using individual learning plans for students to address individual needs, as well as requirements for graduation, and are they effective?

- Is a more individualized system cost effective?

- Would a more individualized system of graduation requirements require more teachers?

- Should all students, regardless of ability level or future plans, be expected to participate in the same curriculum with the same graduation requirements?

- How does the system in our school district work? What is the graduation rate?

- What graduation requirements are in place in schools with a high graduation rate and high-performing students?

- Students may find, after answering pertinent questions, that there is not enough support to prove their thesis, and they may need to revise or change it.

Collecting the Information

Name: _____

Thesis statement for research project:

_____

_____

_____

_____

_____

Write down as many questions as you can think of that would provide answers that support or prove your thesis statement.

_____

_____

_____

_____

_____

_____

_____

_____

_____

Collecting the Information

Share with students that you will be practicing recording only the information that supports your thesis statement. Using the eLibrary article, "More Emphasis on Math, Science: Leaders Rightly Push for Expanded, Rigorous K–12 Programs," record pertinent information on 4 x 6 notecards. (It is recommended that smaller 3x5" cards be used to record bibliographic information.)

Thesis: *In order to be competitive in the job market, American high school students, regardless of ability or future plans, should participate in a challenging curriculum with rigorous graduation requirements.*

Heading to summarize recorded information.   **Bibliography card number.**

Foreign vs. American Students   2

Intel board Chair Craig Barrett said the number of American students qualified for positions in his corporation is small compared to other nations. Asian and European nations require more math and science of their students, and these students often get jobs that require this background.

States Increasing Graduation Requirements   2

In Minnesota, up to 33 percent of future jobs will be in technology. A survey of more than 91,000 eighth through tenth graders last year (2005) showed that only 11 percent of middle school students and 21 percent of tenth graders were interested in jobs in the areas of technology, math, and science.

The Minnesota Legislature and State Dept. of Education created STEM (Science, Technology, Engineering, and Math Initiative) to increase requirements for high school students.

As students record notes, it is important to record bibliographic information from that source at the same time. Students can create a 3x5" card (or section of a notebook page) for each source from which notes are taken. The card for each source should be numbered. The number should be included on any note cards that correspond to that source. By doing this, students can simply sort the note cards alphabetically when ready to create their bibliography. It will also be easy for them to see where they got each piece of information when writing their research paper.

Collecting the Information

Using the bibliographic guidelines, create a bibliography card for the eLibrary article:

2

"More emphasis on math, science: Leaders rightly push for expanded, rigorous K-12 programs." *Minneapolis Star Tribune* (July 23, 2006) eLibrary. Sweetwater County Library, Green River, Wyoming. 6 5 2006 http://elibrary.bigchalk.com

---

The number in the upper right corner shows that this is the second source recorded, and by adding it to the note cards above, shows where the information was found.

Using Graphics As Information

Using a photograph, drawing, graph, or chart can be a better way of expressing ideas than just using text. Graphic information is recorded in the same way as text. Your note card should include a copy of the graphic being used, if possible. If not, include a brief sketch on your card of what the graphic includes, create a bibliography card for it, and assign the appropriate number to the upper right corner of your note card.

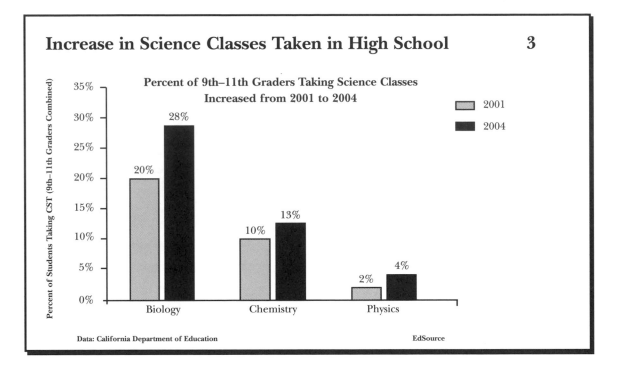

Increase in Science Classes Taken in High School 3

Percent of 9th–11th Graders Taking Science Classes Increased from 2001 to 2004

Data: California Department of Education   EdSource

3

"More High School Students are Taking Science Courses, Particularly Biology. " June, 2005. *EdSource Online.* 18 September 2006. <http://www.edsource.org/sch_hig_scienceclass0104.cfm>

Collecting the Information

Using one informational source you found through your research, create one note card and a bibliography card. Refer to the MLA or APA guidelines your teacher has provided.

Note Card

Bibliography Card

About Note Cards

1. Write only one idea on each note card.

2. Each note card should include:

    a. The specific heading to which the note refers. (As you organize your information, these headings will become your main points and subpoints of your research project.)

    b. Bibliography card number.

    c. Your notes.

    d. The page number (if available) on which you found the information.

3. Take brief notes in your own words. The accuracy of your notes determines the accuracy of the facts in your paper.

4. Quotations should be copied completely and precisely, and enclosed in quotation marks. Make sure you write down the full name of the person who said the quoted information.

About Bibliography Cards

1. Copy the bibliographical information accurately from your informational source using the examples provided by your teacher. This information will be transferred to your bibliography page later.

2. Assign a number to each card, and place it in the upper right hand corner. That way each informational source has a particular number that can be transferred to note cards to quickly pinpoint a source.

3. Write your name on the back of each card so if misplaced, it can be returned to you.

4. When they appear in print, the titles of books, periodicals, films, and television series are italicized. In your handwritten notes, such titles should be underlined. If your project will be created on a computer, italicize appropriate titles.

Organizing the Information

As students research their topics, they begin to find answers to their questions that support or help them prove their research statements. They find that one source of information supports another, which helps confirm the thesis.

When students feel they are nearing the end of the note-taking process, they can begin to sort their note cards by putting similar points together. They may use a graphic organizer to organize their information into main points and supporting points. Generally, in any extensive research project, students should have a minimum of three main points to support the thesis statement. The descriptive headings used on the note cards may become the main points of the project, with the details on the card serving as support for each of these main points or ideas. Students may also use graphics (tables, photos, drawings) to enhance their research. This information (or reference to it) should be included on a card and included in the organizing process.

You may decide to require a graphic organizer as one step in the research process to help students arrange their thoughts in an organized order. Several examples of graphic organizers are included in this section.

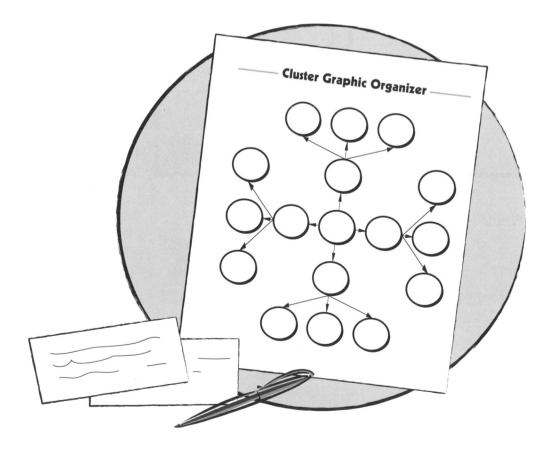

Organizing the Information

Using the thesis statement on high school graduation requirements, complete a graphic organizer with student help. A reproducible page follows. Also, see pages 49–51 for more graphic organizers.

Thesis Statement

In order to be competitive in the job market, American high school students, regardless of ability or future plans, should participate in a challenging curriculum with rigorous graduation requirements.

Main Idea #1	**Main Idea #2**	**Main Idea #3**

Supporting Details:

1.

2.

3.

Supporting Details:

1.

2.

3.

Supporting Details:

1.

2.

3.

Thesis Statement

Main Idea #1	**Main Idea #2**	**Main Idea #3**

Supporting Details:

1.

2.

3.

Supporting Details:

1.

2.

3.

Supporting Details:

1.

2.

3.

Organizing the Information

Student Exercise 1 Worksheet

Using your thesis statement, main points, and supporting details from note cards, complete the graphic organizer.

Thesis Statement

Main Idea #1	Main Idea #2	Main Idea #3

Supporting Details: Supporting Details: Supporting Details:

1.   1.   1.

2.   2.   2.

3.   3.   3.

Outlining

Thesis:

I.   Introductory Paragraph

     A.

     B.

     C.

II.   Supporting Body Paragraph

     A.

     B.

     C.

III.   Supporting Body Paragraph

     A.

     B.

     C.

IV.   Supporting Body Paragraph

     A.

     B.

     C.

V.   Concluding Paragraph

     A.

     B.

     C.

Spider Concept Web

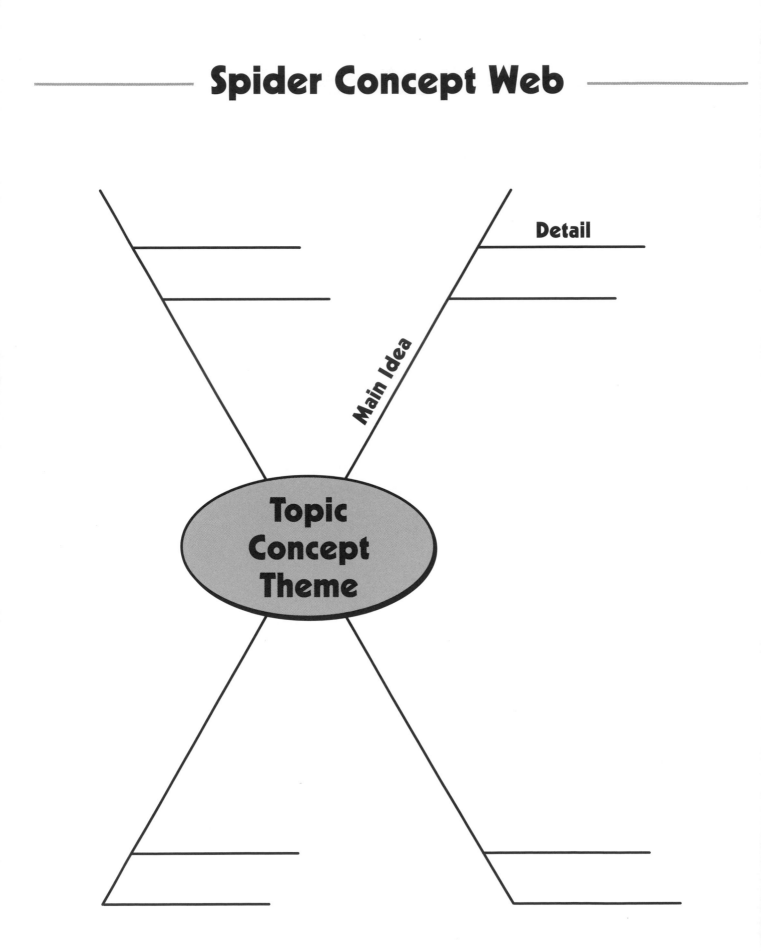

Detail

Main Idea

Topic
Concept
Theme

Cluster Graphic Organizer

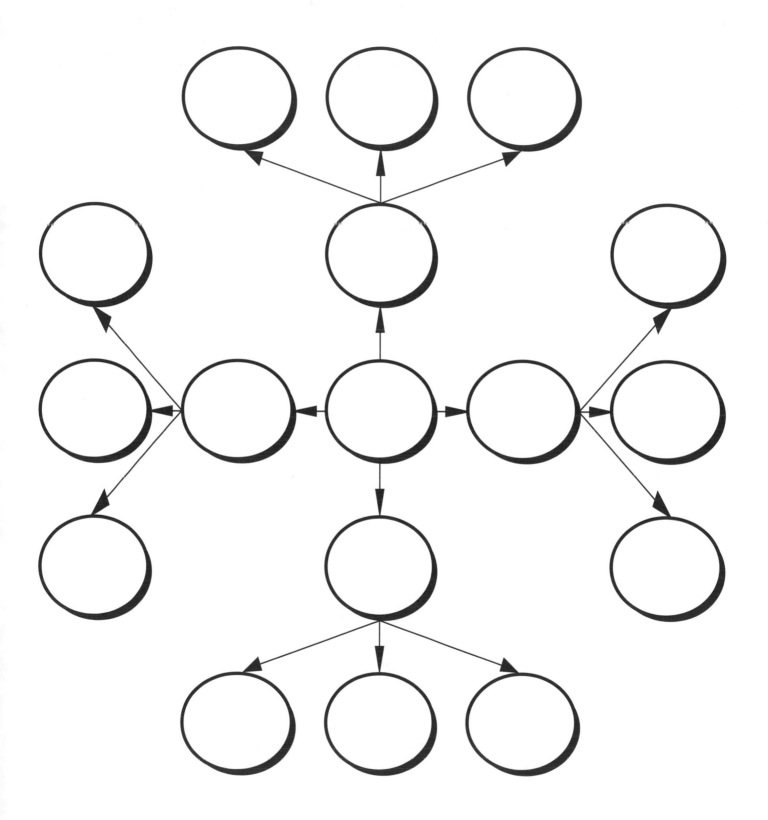

Citing Sources: Giving Credit Where Credit Is Due

Students must always give proper credit for information or ideas from another source that are used in a research project. Credit is given within the text of the project and on a separate page at the end of the project.

Because lengthy bibliographic explanations can be distracting to the reader, the use of parenthetical citations within the text is recommended over the use of footnotes at the end of each page. Likewise, at the end of the project, a bibliography or works cited page is all that is necessary to support the citations within the text.

Standard references for citing in academic research include the MLA (Modern Language Association) and APA (American Psychological Association). MLA is used for writing in the liberal arts area, and the APA is used for citing of scientific research.

This section provides examples of parenthetical citations and preparing a bibliography, works cited, or reference page.

The citation process is one with which students struggle. The citation process should be thought of as no more than another formula that we would use to solve a math problem.

We know the source, and we have a format. It is as simple as transferring our information to the format.

It is important that students understand the importance of citing and practice it often. They can practice using their textbooks, periodical articles, and even their own created works.

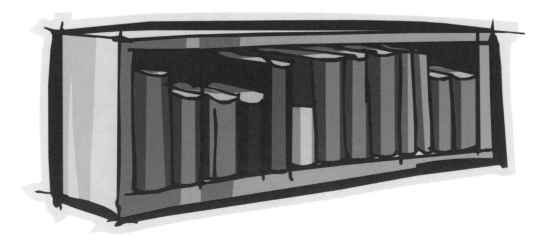

Plagiarism

Plagiarism is using other people's ideas and words without clearly acknowledging the source of that information. When conducting research, you are working with ideas and information created by many authors. It is important to use your own voice when writing about information you think is important and would like to include in your project. When including exact words that the author has used, they must be enclosed with quotation marks with the author's name cited within the text.

To avoid plagiarism, you must give credit whenever you use ...

- another person's idea;

- any facts, statistics, graphs, drawings that are not common knowledge;

- quotations of another person's actual spoken or written words; or

- paraphrase of another person's spoken or written words.

When using electronic information, it is easy to copy and paste information from the original passage into the paper on which you are working. This invites using information that is not in your own words and encourages plagiarism.

In order to prevent plagiarism of material, put **quotation marks around words you have copied exactly from the text** when recording them on note cards. That way you will know exactly where to give the author credit as you copy the quote in your paper. **When you are rewriting information for your research, make sure it is in your own words.** First, read the original passage slowly. Then write your own summary of the passage without using words from the original. Finally, **compare what you have written with the original.** If you have only changed a few words or rearranged sentences, it is plagiarism.

Example of summarized text with an exact quote using a parenthetical citation:

In his book, *The South Beach Diet*, Dr. Agatston examines the history of weight-loss diets during the last forty years. Overweight individuals have been encouraged to eat food high in carbohydrates, food with no carbohydrates, and food high in protein and saturated fats. What has been learned is that "the United States and the northern European countries with the high fat intake and high heart attack rates also had the lowest levels of fiber in their carbohydrates (Agatston, 56)."

In-Text Parenthetical Citations

Direct Quotations

Teacher Modeling Idea 1

Share with students that information that is copied directly from the source should be used when necessary to emphasize a point or convey information in the exact form in which it is stated. These direct quotations should correspond precisely with the originals.

Brief, direct quotations should be included in the regular text of the research paper and enclosed in double quotation marks. The author's last name and page number on which the information can be found should be included in parentheses.

Example of a direct quotation incorporated into the text:

> The last year of high school is a challenge for students, teachers, administrators, and parents. "The composition of today's senior class is much more diverse than a century ago, when only 3 percent of students graduated from high school (Reese 14)."

Longer quotations of two or more sentences should be set off from the text in single spacing. The quotation should be indented five spaces from the left margin, and five spaces from the right margin, with no quotation marks at the beginning or the end. A double space should be allowed between the regular text and the quotation.

Example of a block quotation set apart from the text:

> The myth holds that there were so many Southern sympathizers in Montana that the territory was in danger of pulling out of the Union. The myth was perpetuated in editorials by Montana Post Editor Thomas J. Dimsdale.
>
> > Threats have been made that anyone would be shot who dared to raise the star-spangled banner. What are we to think when drunken horsemen galloping by at midnight often fire random shots at the red, white and blue target while hurrahing lustily for Jeff Davis? (Fritz 54)

Using a book or article of your choice, model this process for students.

In-Text Parenthetical Citations

Alec Bourne wrote about schools and education. His quote: "It is entirely possible to store the mind with a million facts and still be entirely uneducated." *Dictionary of Quotations*, p. 38.

J. K. Rowling writes Harry Potter books. Her quote: "Hearing voices no one else can hear isn't a good sign even in the wizarding world." From *Harry Potter and the Chamber of Secrets*, p. 192.

Using one of the quotes above, create an accurate in-text citation that could be used in a writing assignment:

Now, use an example from one of your note cards, and create a direct quote in-text citation:

Citing Sources:
Giving Credit Where Credit is Due

Especially with younger students, it might be beneficial to practice writing a very basic bibliographic citation. Using a student's own work in citation writing practice can help students understand the importance of the process and perhaps help them better understand what a citation is.

Create an original book by folding an 8½ x 11" sheet of paper in half so it resembles covers of a book. On the front of the book, write the title and your name as the author. You may use a personal piece of writing or something you made up. On the inside, right-hand page, again write your title, and your name as author. This will be your "title page." At the bottom of the page, write the name of the publishing company, and the city and state where the book was published. Again, use your creativity. On the back of the title page, write the copyright symbol, followed by the publication date.

Then, model for students, what the citation would look like based on your personal "book," by writing it on an overhead, whiteboard, etc.

Citing Sources:
Giving Credit Where Credit is Due

Directions: You will create a book cover and title page for a piece of personal writing. This could be a poem or short story you have created.

Using an 8½ x 11" sheet of paper, fold the page in half.

On the front page, design the cover of your book by writing your title, your name as the author, and an illustration or design.

Open the page, and on the right-hand side, create your title page. This page should include your title and your name. At the bottom of the page, write the name of the publishing company and the city and state where your book was published. Be creative.

Turn the page so you are looking at the last page or back page. At the top of this page, write the copyright symbol, followed by the year your book was published.

When you are finished, write the bibliographic citation for your book in the space below:

List of Works Cited

Most style manuals require you to assemble a list of the works that you have cited in your paper. This list, included at the end of your paper, may be termed Works Cited, a Reference List, or a Bibliography. Offered here are some of the most commonly used forms of cited material in both MLA and APA style.

MLA Style

Book – One Author

Gardner, Howard. <u>Multiple Intelligences</u>. New York: Basic Books, 1993.

Book – Two or More Authors

Lundin, Stephen, Harry Paul, and John Christensen. <u>Fish!</u> New York: Hyperion, 2000.

Book – Edited

Peary, Danny, Ed. <u>We Played the Game</u>. New York: Hyperion, 1994.

Encyclopedias and Other Multi-Volumed Work

Lumiansky, R.M. "Tolstoy." <u>The New Encyclopaedia Britannica: Macropaedia</u>. 15th ed. 1998.

Magazine Article – Print Format

Einhorn, Bruce and Ben Elgin. "Helping Big Brother Go High Tech." <u>Business Week</u> 18 Sept. 2006: 46–52.

Journal Article – Print Format

Hoffert, Barbara. "The United Way." *Library Journal* 8 (2006): 38–41.

APA Style

Book – One Author

Gardner, H. (1993) *Multiple intelligences.* New York: Basic Books.

Book – Two or More Authors

Lundin, S., H. Paul, and J. Christensen. (2000) *Fish!* New York: Hyperion.

Book – Edited

Peary, D, E., ed. (1994) *We played the game.* New York: Hyperion.

Encyclopedias and Other Multi-Volumed Work

Lumiansky, R.M. (1998). Tolstoy. In *The new encyclopaedia britannica: Macropaedia.* (15, p 745–748). Chicago: Encyclopedia Britannica.

Magazine Article – Print Format

Einhorn, B. and Elgin, B. (2006 Sept. 18) Helping big brother go high tech. *Business Week,* 46: 38–41.

Journal Article – Print Format

Hoffert, B. (2006) "The united way." *Library Journal,* 8, 38–41.

MLA Style

Magazine Article from an Online Database

Castleman, Michael. "Herbal First Aid." <u>Mother Earth News</u>. Mar/Apr 2005. EBSCOHost. Sweetwater County Library, Green River, Wy. September 2006 <u>http://web.ebscohost.com</u>

Newspaper Article from an Online Database

Herzehorn, David M. "An Unfailing Belief in the Power of Teaching." <u>New York Times</u>. 26 July 2006, <u>EBSCO Masterfile Premier</u>, Mansfield Library, Univ. of Montana, Missoula. 17 Sept. 2006 <u>http://web.ebscohost.com</u>

Website

<u>National Weather Service</u>. 17 Sept. 2006. National Oceanic and Atmospheric Administration. 17 Sept. 2006 <u>http://www.nws.noaa.gov</u>

An Interview That You Conducted

Smith, James. Personal Interview. 8 Aug. 2006. Muncie, Indiana.

APA Style

Magazine Article from an Online Database

Castleman, M. (2005, Mar/Apr) Herbal first aid. *Mother Earth News*. Retrieved September 18, 2006, from *EBSCOHost* database.

Newspaper Article from an Online Database

Herzehorn, D. M. (2006, July 26) An unfailing belief in the power of teaching. *New York Times*. Retrieved Sept. 17, 2006 from *EBSCO Masterfile Premier* database.

Website

National Oceanic and Atmospheric Administration. (2006, Sept. 17). *National Weather Service*. Retrieved September 17, 2006 from <u>http://www.nws.noaa.gov</u>

An Interview That You Conducted

Smith, James. (2006, Aug. 8). Personal Interview. Muncie, Indiana.

For additional information on citing various sources, refer to the following:

<u>MLA Handbook for Writers of Research Papers</u>. 6th ed. New York: Modern Language Association of America, 2003; and <u>Publication Manual of the American Psychological Association</u>. 5th ed. Washington: American Psychological Association, 2001.

Citing Sources:
Giving Credit Where Credit Is Due
Creating a Bibliographic Citation

Teacher Modeling Idea 3

Share with students that you are going to create a short bibliography or works cited page together. Use a book with which students are familiar—a textbook or novel. Using the MLA style guidelines, create an entry for your bibliography.

Textbook or novel:

Next share a printed copy of an article from a popular magazine. Create a bibliographic entry for this title.

Magazine:

Citing Sources:
Giving Credit Where Credit Is Due

Using two different types of informational sources in which you have found research material, create a bibliographic entry for each. Use the MLA style guidelines to complete your entries.

Entry 1

Entry 2

Putting It All Together

Perhaps the most exciting, but often the most difficult, step of the research project is connecting the information together so that it serves its intended purpose of solving an informational problem. Bringing all of the ideas and components together to create a new product is called synthesis. All pieces must be in place to form a complete, new creation.

Any integrated project that is worth doing is worth doing well. Students need time to learn and practice prerequisite skills needed for carrying out a sophisticated research project, and they need time to complete their project in a quality manner. Allow adequate class time for this work to be accomplished. Students should also have access to technology and specialized staff such as the media specialist and technology teacher.

As students analyze their work, they must align what they have done with the rubric and sample projects you examined with them when the project was first introduced. In this final stage of project development, examine the rubric together one more time, discussing what is expected from each component for a quality product.

Depending on the project format students have been assigned or have selected to use, their finished product should contain the same final steps and information. These will be examined in this section.

Final Steps of the Research Process

Regardless of the format students select to present their research, all projects should include the following:

1) **A title page**

2) **Acknowledgements page**

3) **The body of research**

4) **A works cited page or bibliography**

5) **A works consulted page**

A written title page must be included in any research project. Whether the student is preparing a PowerPoint, an oral presentation, or written paper, a title page must accompany all formats. The title page should include the title, student's name, teacher's name, course name, and the date submitted.

Sample Title Page

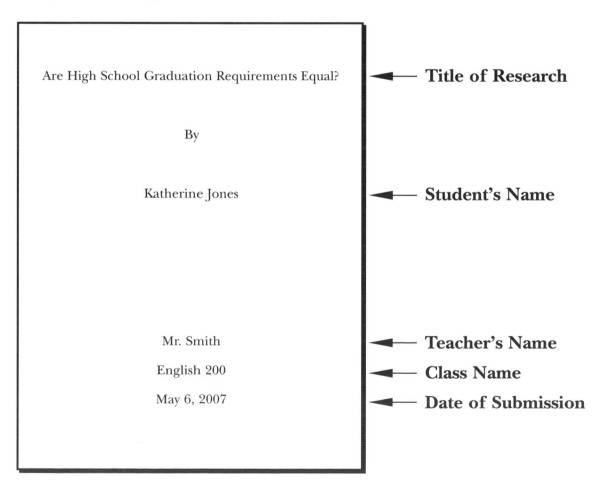

Are High School Graduation Requirements Equal?	◄— **Title of Research**
By	
Katherine Jones	◄— **Student's Name**
Mr. Smith	◄— **Teacher's Name**
English 200	◄— **Class Name**
May 6, 2007	◄— **Date of Submission**

Acknowledgements Page

An acknowledgements page is a location to recognize individuals who offered assistance in the research process. This could be school staff members who offered assistance, such as a media specialist or computer teacher. This would be an appropriate place to thank someone for granting a personal interview. It could also be a thank you to an author whose work provided inspiration to the student to research a particular topic. Although this could be an optional requirement, it provides an opportunity for a student to express gratitude for special assistance in his/her area of research.

Sample Acknowledgements Page

Example 1:

I would like to thank Mrs. Bernard, media specialist, for assisting me in locating resources for my research paper. Mrs. McClure, computer lab manager, was also very helpful in allowing me time to work on my PowerPoint presentation.

Example 2:

I would like to thank Mr. Doug Coleton for the tour of the Fish and Game Office, which provided a valuable insight into my research on endangered wildlife.

Example 3:

I would like to extend a special thanks to Suzanne Metzinger, who provided a personal interview to discuss graduation requirements in our school district. Learning about our local district helped me to better understand the articles I read from other areas.

The Body of Research

The presentation of research results is just as important as conducting the research. Students may have read through pages of information and taken copious notes, but unless they can present it effectively, they have not been successful in their endeavor. In order to have a meaningful presentation, students must be competent in the mode they have chosen to express their information. If they put their results in writing, they must understand what good research writing looks like; if they present orally, they must have a clear idea of what effective speaking sounds like because they have seen it modeled, and have had an opportunity to practice those skills. When students are integrating their information and creating their presentation, it is another opportunity to revisit the rubric and discuss expectations for this portion of the project. Tips for student presentation of information are included in the next section.

Documentation of Sources Pages

Teachers will specify which type of bibliographic page(s) is required. The following offers a definition for each page type.

Works Cited Page

The works cited page includes an alphabetical, bibliographic list of all work that has been cited within the text of a research paper.

Bibliography

A bibliography page is an alphabetical, bibliographic list of all references that a student has used for research, including both cited references and those used for information but not cited within the text.

Works Consulted Page

A works consulted page includes references that were used for information, but not cited within the text.

Guidelines for Creating Works Cited, Bibliography, and Works Consulted Pages in MLA style

- Center the title (such as "Works Cited") at the top of the page.

- All entries should be single-spaced.

- A double space should occur between each entry.

- Begin an entry at the margin; indent the remaining lines five spaces.

- Underline titles of books, periodicals, films, and television series.

Works Cited

Einhorn, Bruce and Ben Elgin. "Helping Big Brother Go High Tech." Business Week 18 Sept. 2006: 46–41

Gardner, Howard. Multiple Intelligences. New York: Basic Books, 1993.

Herzehorn, David M. "An Unfailing Belief in the Power of Teaching," New York Times. 26 July 2006, EBSCO Masterfile Premier, Mansfield Library, Univ. of Montana, Missoula, 17 Sept. 2006 <http://web.ebscohost.com>

Peary, Danny, Ed. We Played the Game. New York: Hyperion, 1994.

Guidelines for Creating Works Cited, Bibliography, and Works Consulted Pages in APA style

- Center the title (such as "Works Cited") at the top of the page.

- All entries should be single-spaced.

- A double space should occur between each entry.

- Begin an entry at the margin; indent the remaining lines five spaces.

- Italicize titles of books, periodicals, films, and television series.

Works Cited

Einhorn, Bruce and Ben Elgin. "Helping Big Brother Go High Tech." *Business Week* 18 Sept. 2006: 46–41

Gardner, Howard. *Multiple Intelligences.* New York: Basic Books, 1993.

Herzehorn, David M. "An Unfailing Belief in the Power of Teaching," New York Times. 26 July 2006, *EBSCO Masterfile Premier*, Mansfield Library, Univ. of Montana, Missoula, 17 Sept. 2006 <http://web.ebscohost.com>

Peary, Danny, Ed. *We Played the Game.* New York: Hyperion, 1994.

Presenting the Research

A variety of choices are available for presenting research results. Students may use writing, graphics, a speech or song, or a multimedia presentation to share the results of their work.

Students have the opportunity to use technology to help organize their research. Through word processing programs, databases, and spreadsheets, information can be typed, sorted, and organized in graphic form. Students may also use various software applications, such as PowerPoint, Web page design, and graphics programs to present their research findings. These choices may allow students effective options in presenting their particular information.

Whatever presentation form is used to share results, the same high expectations apply to all. This section provides tips for students on various forms of presentation.

Tips for a Written Presentation of Results

Writing the Introduction

The introduction is shaped like a funnel with the wide opening at the top. Begin with a general statement about the topic. Follow that with three to five sentences that narrow the focus. And finally, end the opening paragraph with the thesis statement—one sentence stating the main idea of the paper.

The body of the paper includes several paragraphs with information that supports your thesis sentence. Each paragraph is actually its own body. Each one should begin with a transition sentence, or topic sentence, that clearly connects it to the thesis statement. Several sentences follow that provide details that support this topic sentence. Some of this "evidence" may include statistics, direct quotes, and examples that serve to support and clarify the topic sentence and the thesis statement. It is important to cite any statistics or ideas that are used that are not common knowledge.

Each additional paragraph in the body of the paper should include a transition that connects it to the paragraph that precedes it. These transition sentences create a comfortable flow that occurs in papers that are well organized around the thesis statement.

Each paragraph has an end sentence that briefly summarizes or reinforces the connection between the point being made in the paragraph and the thesis statement of the overall paper.

The final part of the research paper is the conclusion. This paragraph does the opposite of the introductory paragraph. It begins with much-narrowed statement that is your thesis restated. It emphasizes the evidence presented in the body, and ends with a general statement about the topic—just like the opening paragraph began. No new information is introduced in the final paragraph!

Let Your Voice Be Heard!

It is important that the paper be written in the your own words and thoughts. You should write to persuade your audience and show enthusiasm for the topic and the results.

Writing Checklist for Students:

- Does my introductory paragraph funnel from a general statement and end with my thesis statement or main idea of my paper?

- Does my voice let my reader know what my stance is on my topic?

- Does each paragraph in the body of the paper begin with a clear topic sentence that states the paragraph's main idea?

- Does each paragraph connect to the previous one with a transitional word or phrase?

- Does my conclusion state what I have shown through my evidence in the body of my paper and funnel back to a general statement?

- When read aloud, does my paper flow and show logical organization and evidence to prove my thesis?

Be Your Own Editor!

- Begin writing early so you have plenty of time to revise.

- It is helpful to have someone else read your paper aloud (or record it yourself and listen) to check for organization, word choice, and good transitions.

- After completing the final editing for content, check spelling and grammar. Software for checking spelling and grammar does not always catch everything.

- Consistently use the documentation format (MLA or APA) for citing sources that your teacher has specified.

Tips for an Oral Presentation of Results

When you present for an audience, you are performing. Your delivery is your presentation. Practice your speech several times, so you are very familiar and comfortable with what you are going to say. Dress appropriately. Look enthusiastic and confident. Speak slowly and clearly. Speak to the person in the back of the room so everyone is able to hear.

- Body language is a big part of an oral presentation.

- Speak with confidence so it is obvious you really believe what you are saying.

- Take your time. Do not rush yourself or your audience. Give them time to reflect on what you are saying.

- Do not read from notes unless you need to refer to statistics that are difficult to remember. It is important to hold your head up and look at your audience, so everyone can hear what you have to say.

- Look at your audience while you are speaking.

- Add humor when appropriate.

- When using audio-visual supports, make sure everything is working properly before you begin.

- If you have handouts to share, arrange for someone to pass them out at the appropriate time.

- If questions are appropriate, ask for questions at the end of your speech.

- Know when to stop talking if you have been given a time limit.

Tips for Multimedia Presentations

When presenting research results using a multimedia production, the product should be well organized and include all main points and evidence that would be included in a written presentation. Creating a multimedia presentation requires selecting a layout that shares your information effectively, and thus is one step beyond a written paper.

The following checklist will assist in creating a quality presentation:

The Visual Component:

- All material should be completely proofread.

- Information should be well researched, well written, well organized, and created in your own voice.

- Information should show a strong understanding of major ideas and display evidence to support them in a manner that is easily understood by the audience.

- The presentation should have a title page, a bibliography, or works cited page that follows the required citation format (MLA or APA).

- The presentation should include a minimum of 10 slides or frames.

- The presentation should include a variety of text, graphics, transitions, and sound that communicates and complements information.

- The presentation should look professional with an overall theme that effectively communicates the information being shared.

The Oral Component:

- The information should be narrated, rather than simply read, as the multimedia product is being shown.

- The speech and graphics should provide smooth transitions from one main point to another.

- Time should be utilized effectively.

The Technical Component:

- Equipment and software should be in working order and checked ahead of time to avoid any unnecessary problems.

Evaluating the Work

We want to help students become independent learners and effective users of information. Therefore, students need to evaluate their work throughout the entire research process. This is why we began with the end in mind. Students need to be familiar with the rubric upon which their evaluation will be based.

This must be modeled for them at the onset of the project, so it is very clear what the expectations are. Again, it is difficult for any of us to produce quality work if we are just told what to do without teacher modeling and a chance to practice the skills needed. The rubric must be a ready tool that is constantly used by the student as a measuring tape of progress.

Students should examine two components when evaluating the research process. They should evaluate *their project*—the product itself and the presentation. Did the project meet the criteria at a proficient level? Secondly, they need to evaluate *their work* on the project. Was time used wisely? What would they do differently next time?

Evaluating the Work

Share the evaluation form on the following page with students, and explain that you are going to walk through the evaluation process with a sample research project. Choose an anonymous research paper that has already been evaluated by a student in another class. Put the evaluation form on an overhead projector and refer to parts of the paper where the student feels he/she excelled and a part where he/she needed more work.

Discuss the following questions based on the sample project before you ask students to evaluate their own work.

Process:

Was there anything I did not understand about the task asked of me?

What did I learn about the research process while working on my project?

What parts of the project did I find the most difficult? Why?

What would I do differently next time?

Product:

Did my finished project/presentation meet the requirements of the assignment? Why or why not?

What part of my project shows my greatest strength?

What would I do differently next time?

My Effort:

Did I do the best quality work that I could?

What would I do differently next time?

What did I enjoy most about the research process?

Student Evaluation

Please answer the following questions as completely as possible.

Process:

Was there anything I did not understand about the task asked of me? _____

_____

_____

What did I learn about the research process while working on my project? _____

_____

_____

What parts of the project did I find the most difficult? Why? _____

_____

_____

What would I do differently next time? _____

_____

Product:

Did my finished project/presentation meet the requirements of the assignment?
Why or why not? _____

_____

What part of my project shows my greatest strength? _____

_____

What would I do differently next time? _____

_____

My Effort:

Did I do the best quality work that I could? _____

What would I do differently next time? _____

_____

What did I enjoy most about the research process? _____

_____

Additional Resources

American Association of School Librarians. "AASL Standards for the Twenty-First Century Learner." American Association of School Librarians Website. Sept. 7, 2008, http://www.noodletools.com.

MLA Handbook for Writers of Research Papers. 6th ed. New York: Modern Language Association of America, 2003.

Noodle Tools, Inc. Noodle Tools. http://www.noodletools.com. (An online tool to create a bibliography.)

OCLA Online Computer Library Center. A Research Guide for Students. 2008. http://www.aresearchguide.com.

The OWL (Online Writing Lab) at Purdue. Purdue University. http://owl.english.purdue.edu/owl, 2008.

Publication Manual of the American Psychological Association. 5th ed. Washington: American Psychological Association, 2001.